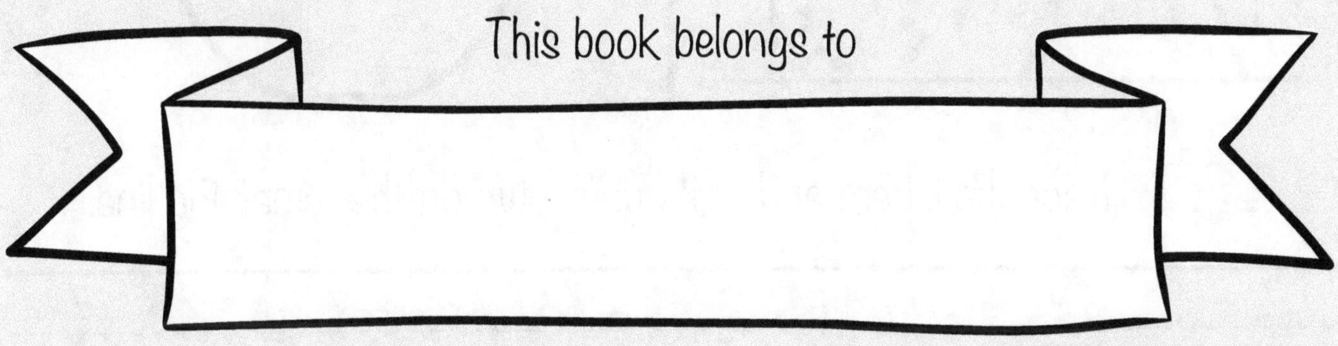

This book belongs to

Videos, music, books, t-shirts and much more can be found on our website

www.CHARELLO-KIDS.com

Aa

Apple
Color the apple

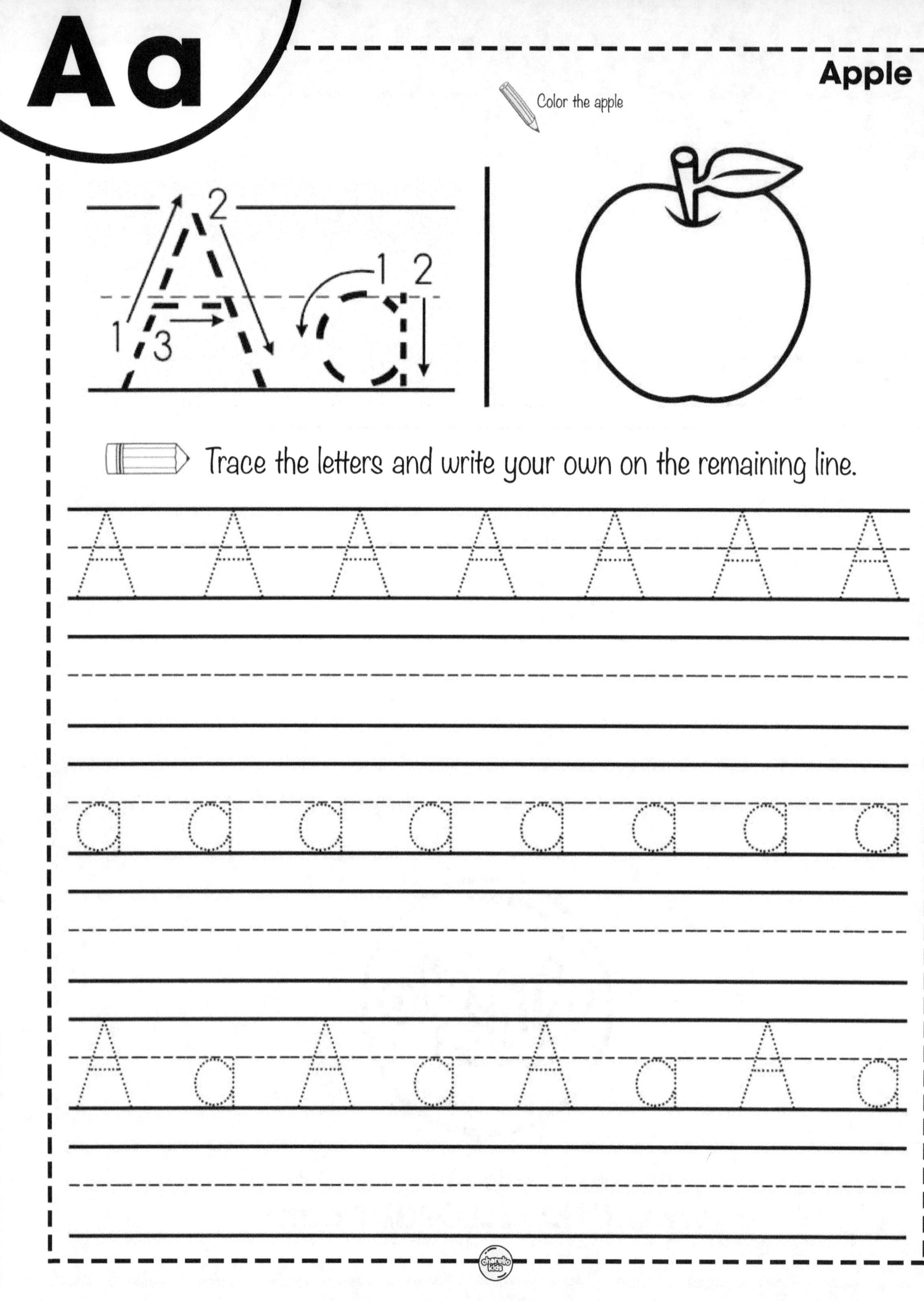

Trace the letters and write your own on the remaining line.

Charello kids

B b

Color the butterfly

Trace the letters and write your own on the remaining line.

Cc

Trace the letters and write your own on the remaining line.

C C C C C C C

C C C C C C C

C C C C C C C

C C C C C C C

C C C C C C C

C C C C C C C

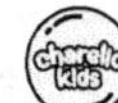

Dd

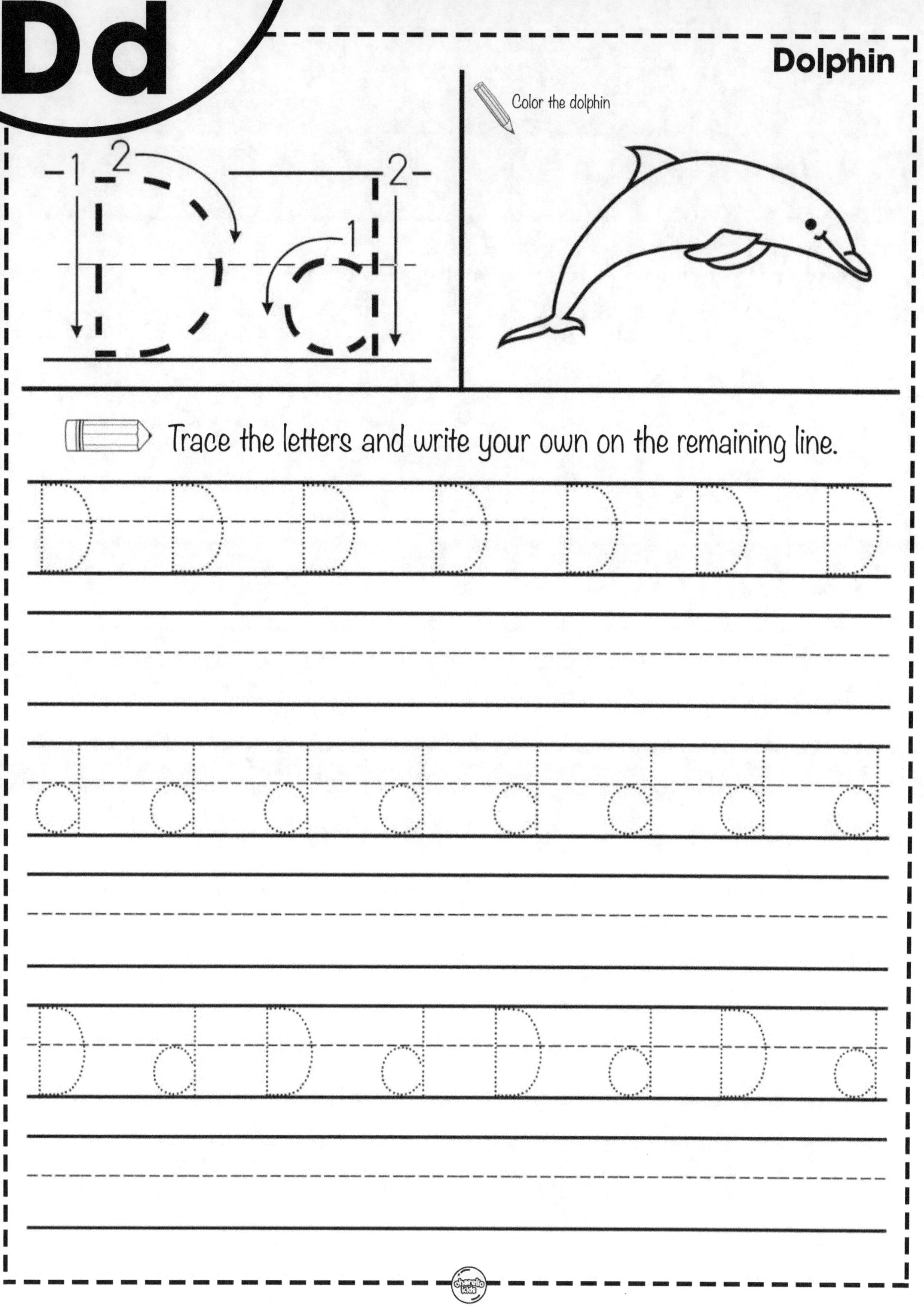

Dolphin
Color the dolphin
Trace the letters and write your own on the remaining line.

Ee

Trace the letters and write your own on the remaining line.

F f

Color the fish

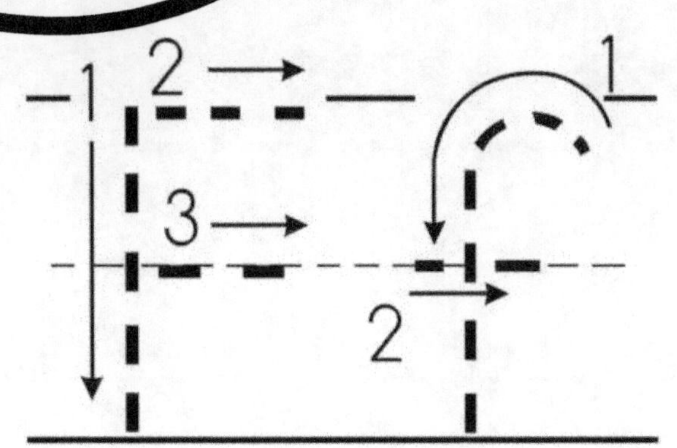

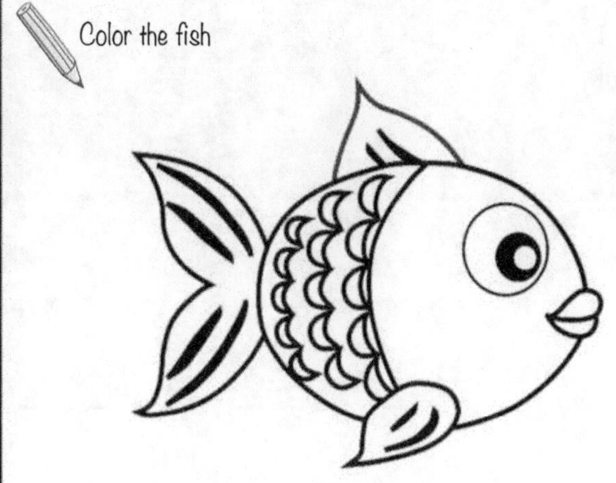

Trace the letters and write your own on the remaining line.

f f f f f f f

f f f f f f f

f f f f f f f

f f f f f f f

f f f f f f f

f f f f f f f

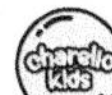

Gg

Giraffe
Color the giraffe
Trace the letters and write your own on the remaining line.

G G G G G G G
G G G G G G G
G G G G G G G
G G G G G G G
G G G G G G G
G G G G G G G

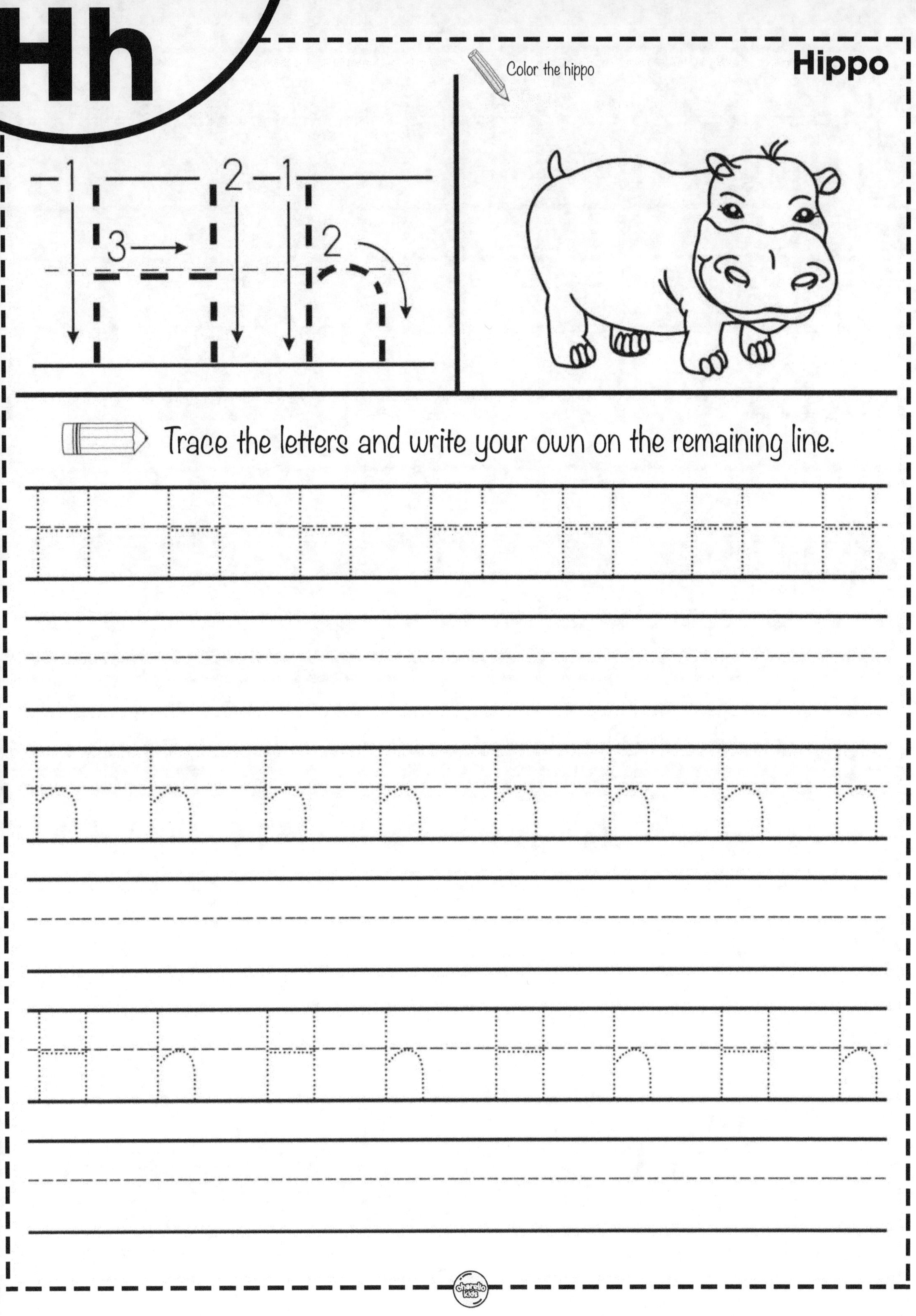

Hh
Color the hippo
Hippo
1
2
1
3
2
Trace the letters and write your own on the remaining line.

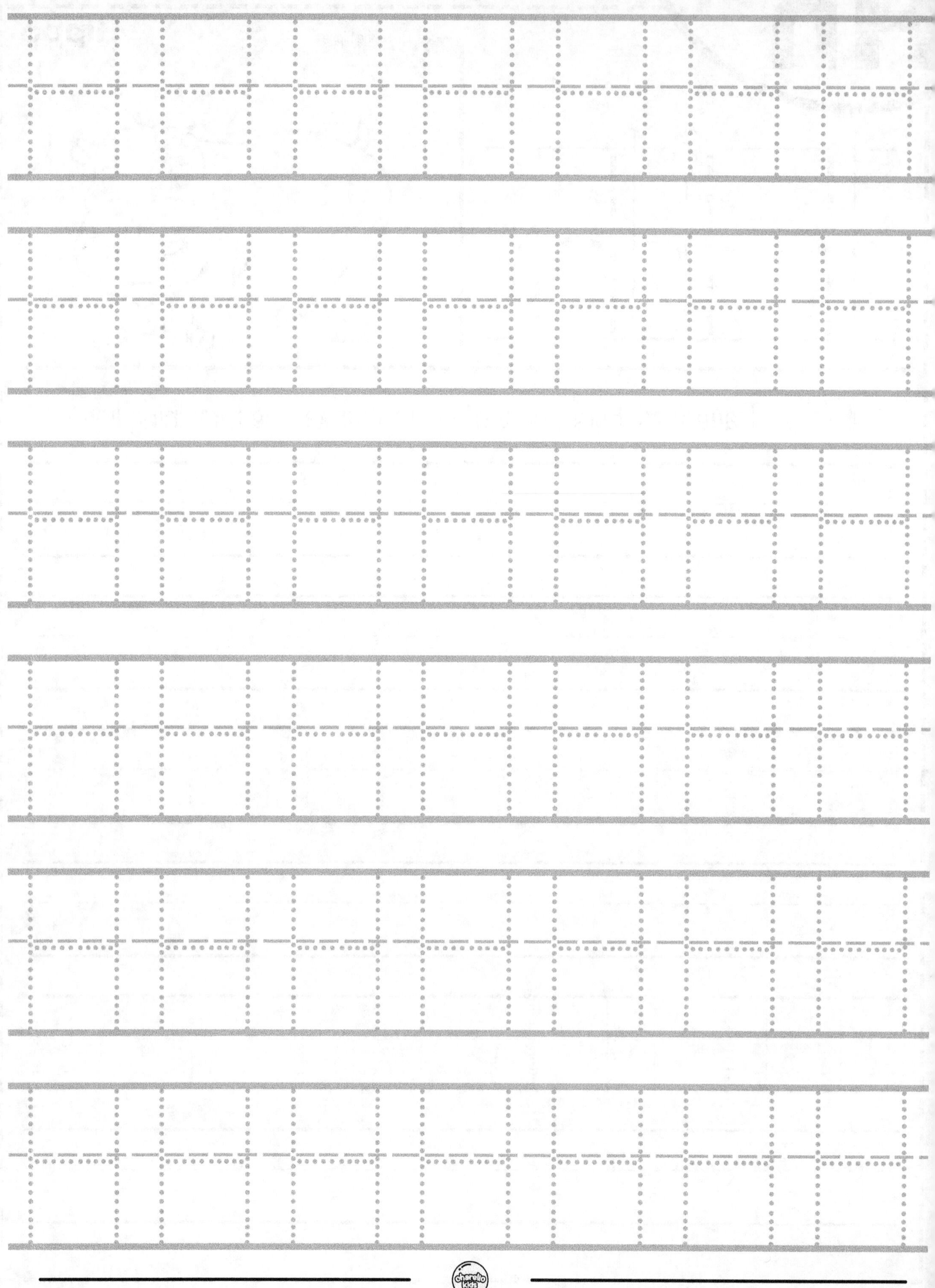

h h h h h h h

h h h h h h h

h h h h h h h

h h h h h h h

h h h h h h h

h h h h h h h

I i

2 →
1
1 ●

3 →

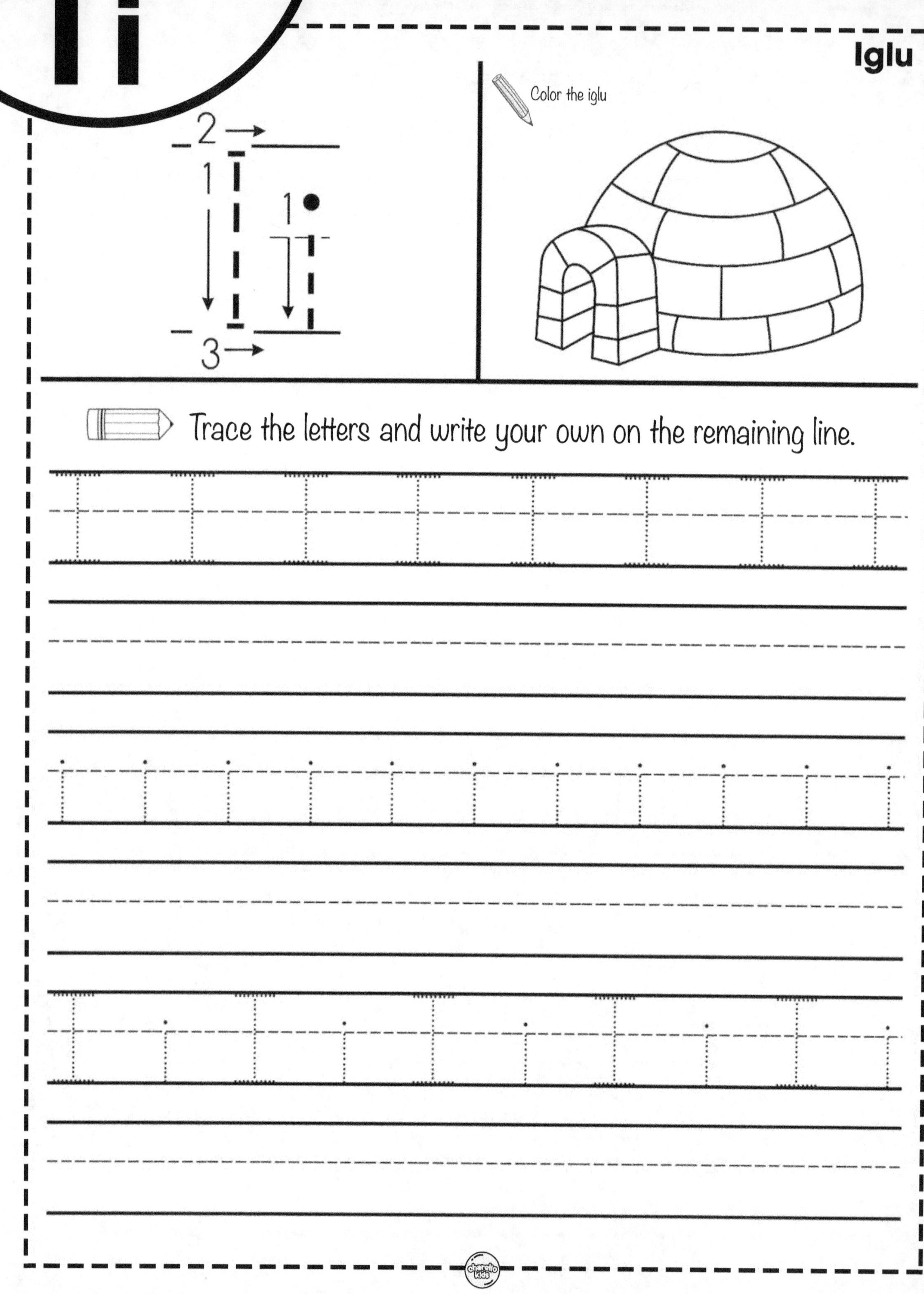

Trace the letters and write your own on the remaining line.

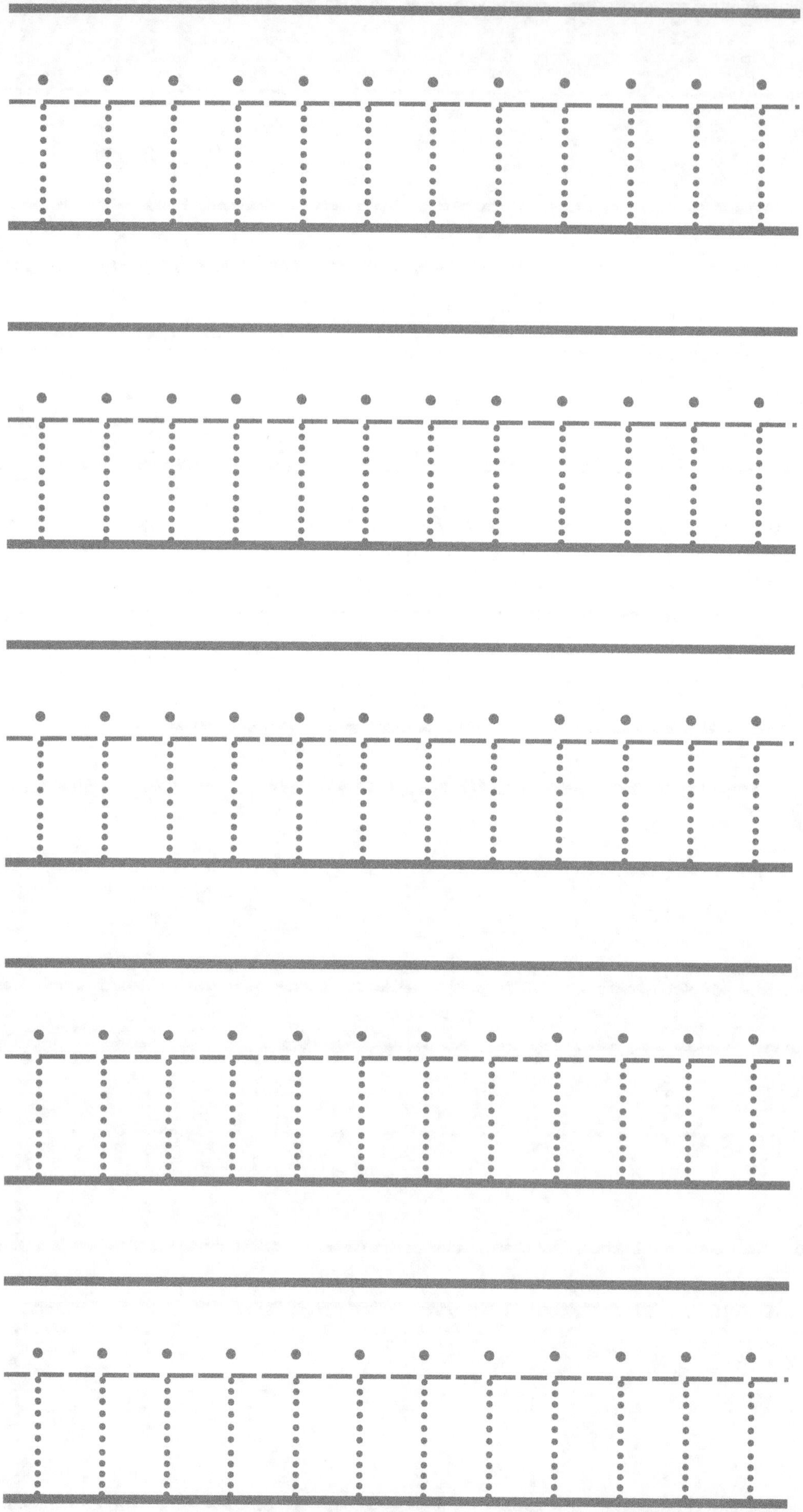

Jj

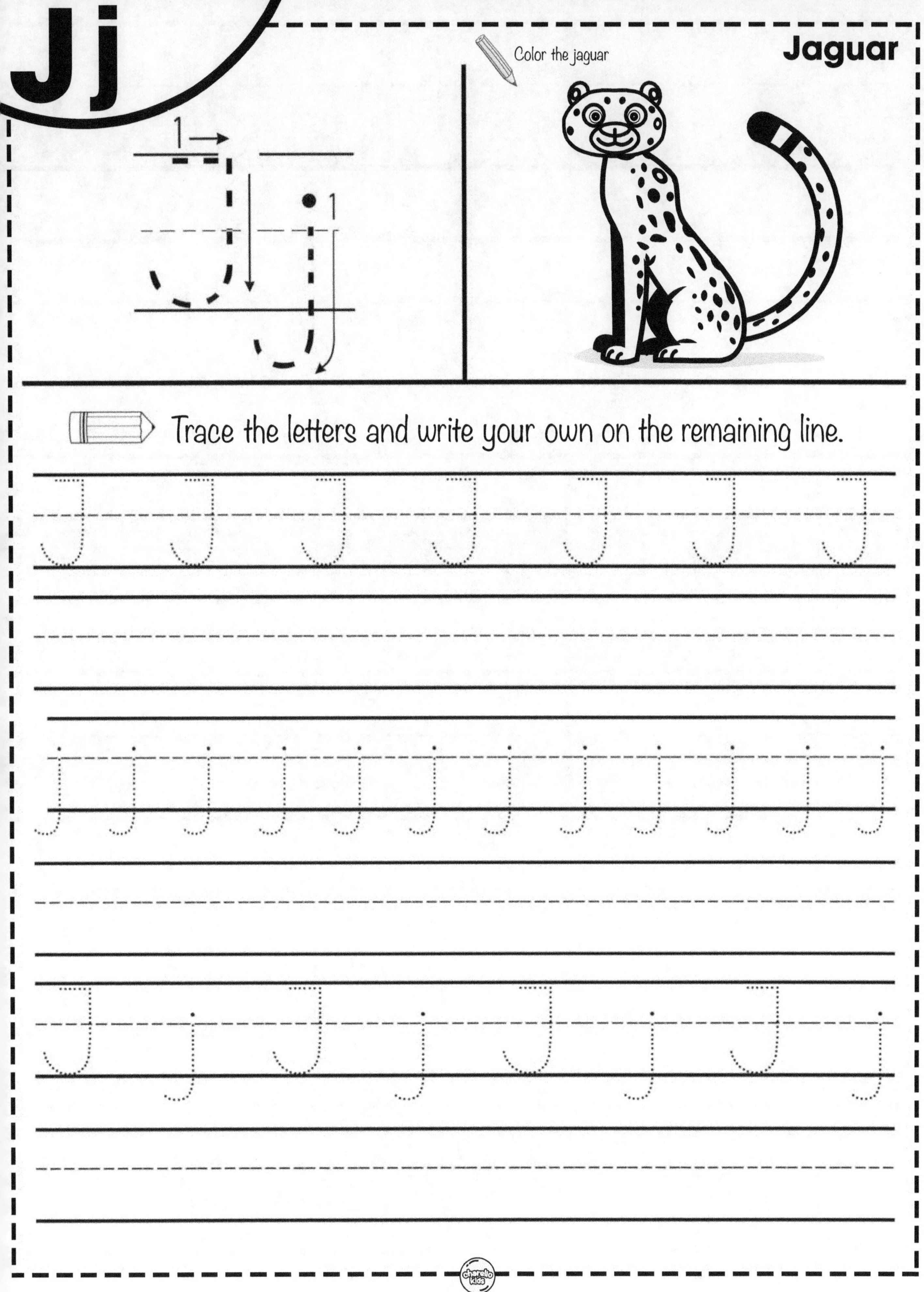

Color the jaguar
1
1
Trace the letters and write your own on the remaining line.
Charelio kids

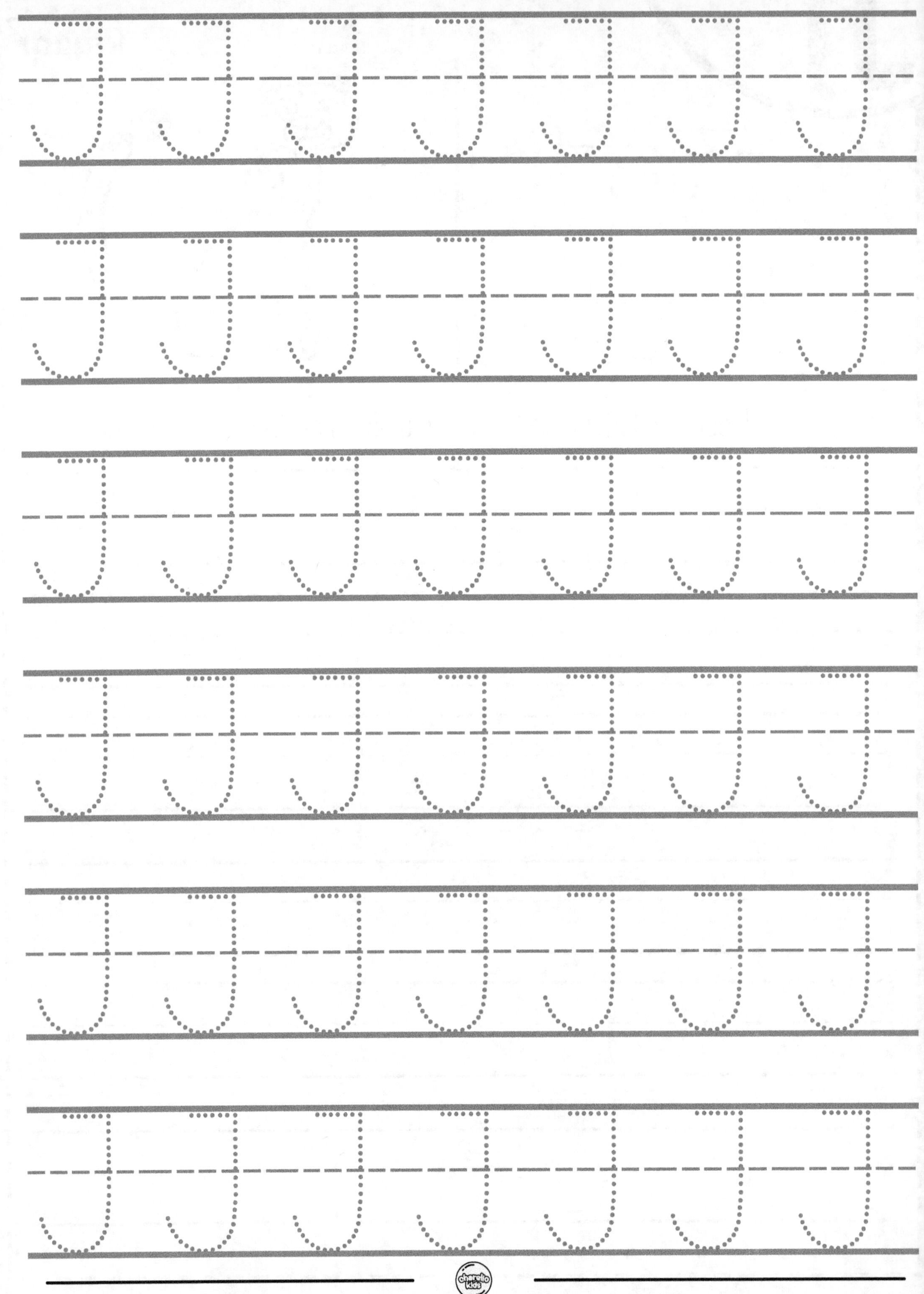

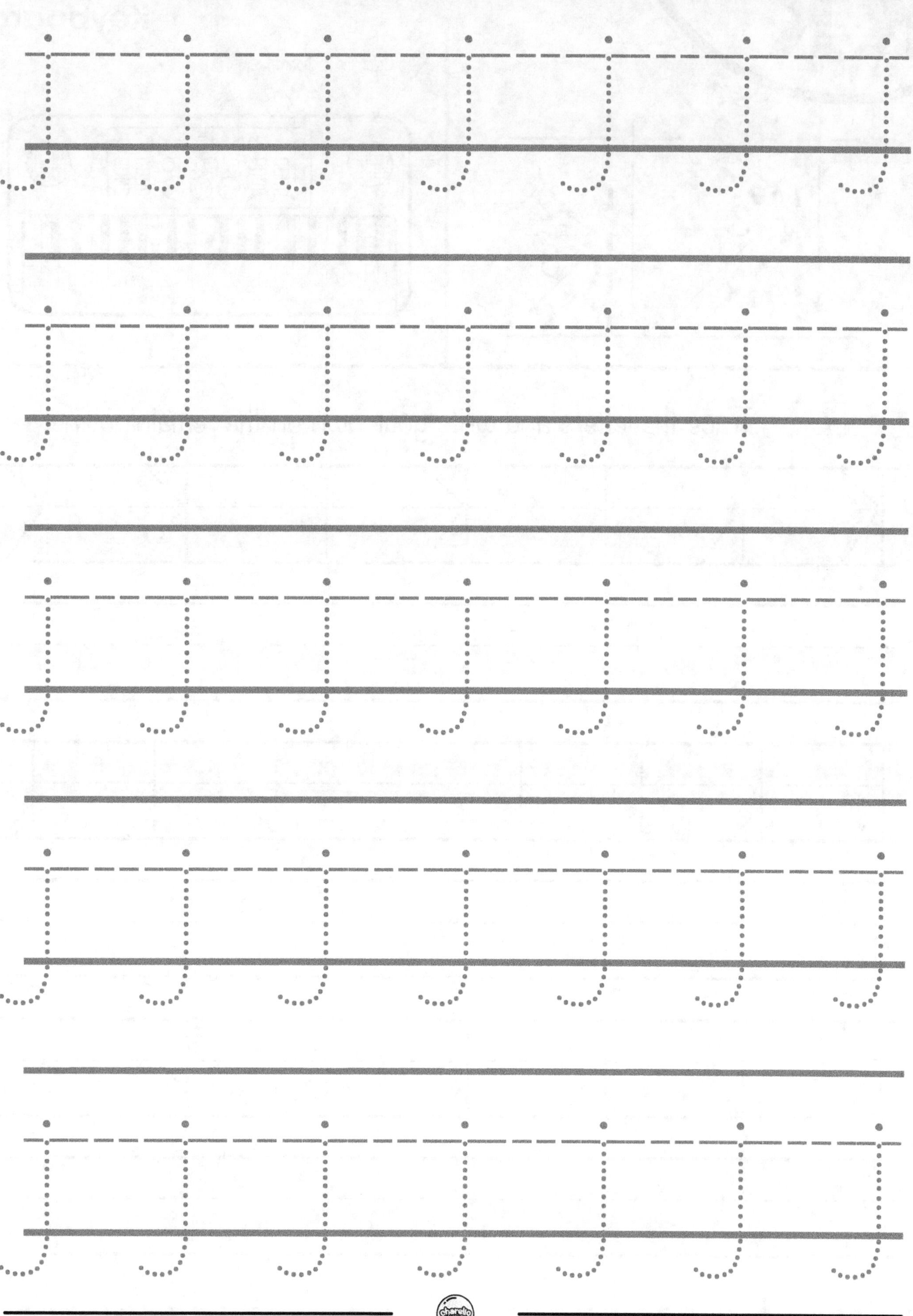

Kk

Color the keyboard
Trace the letters and write your own on the remaining line.

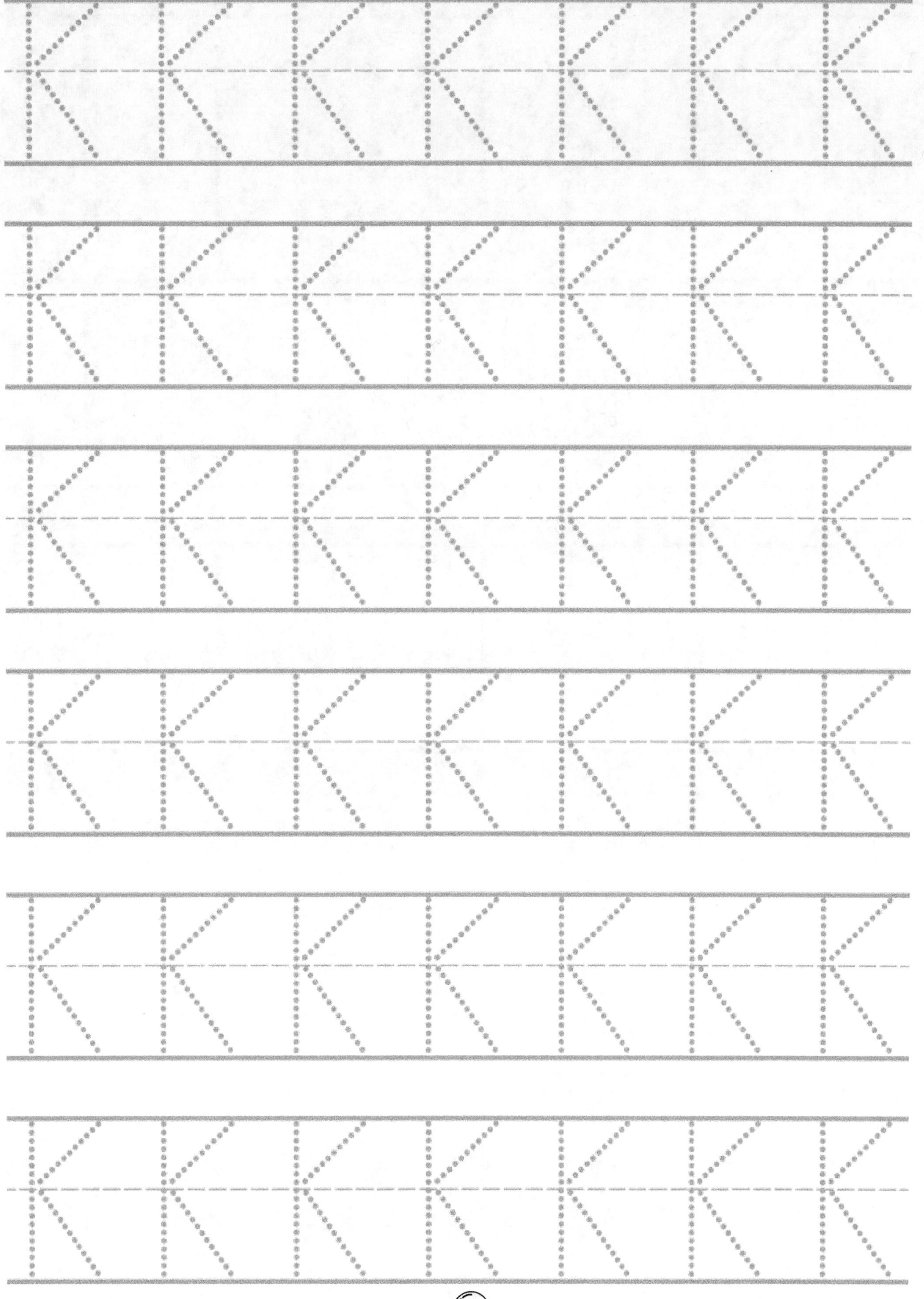

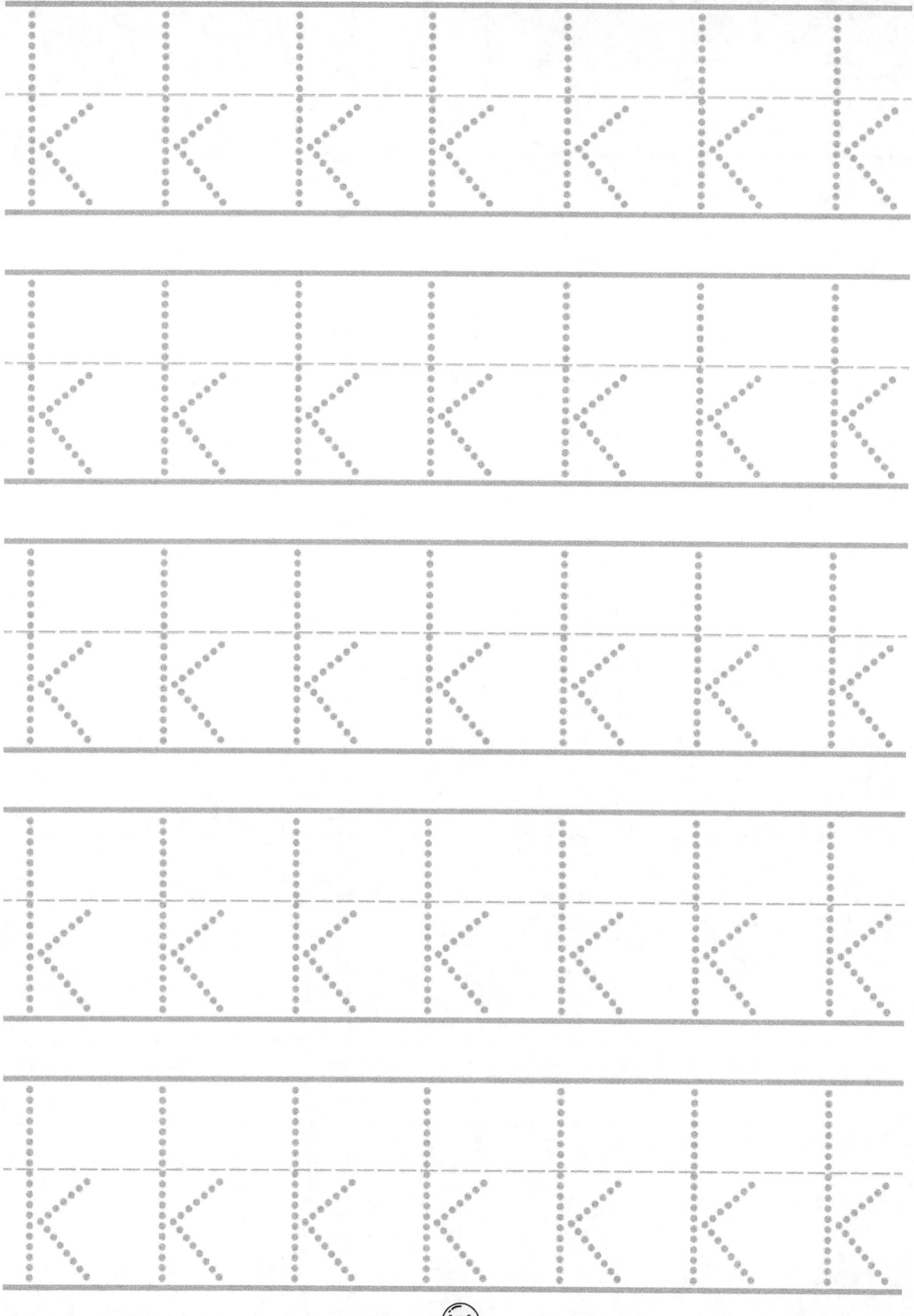

LI

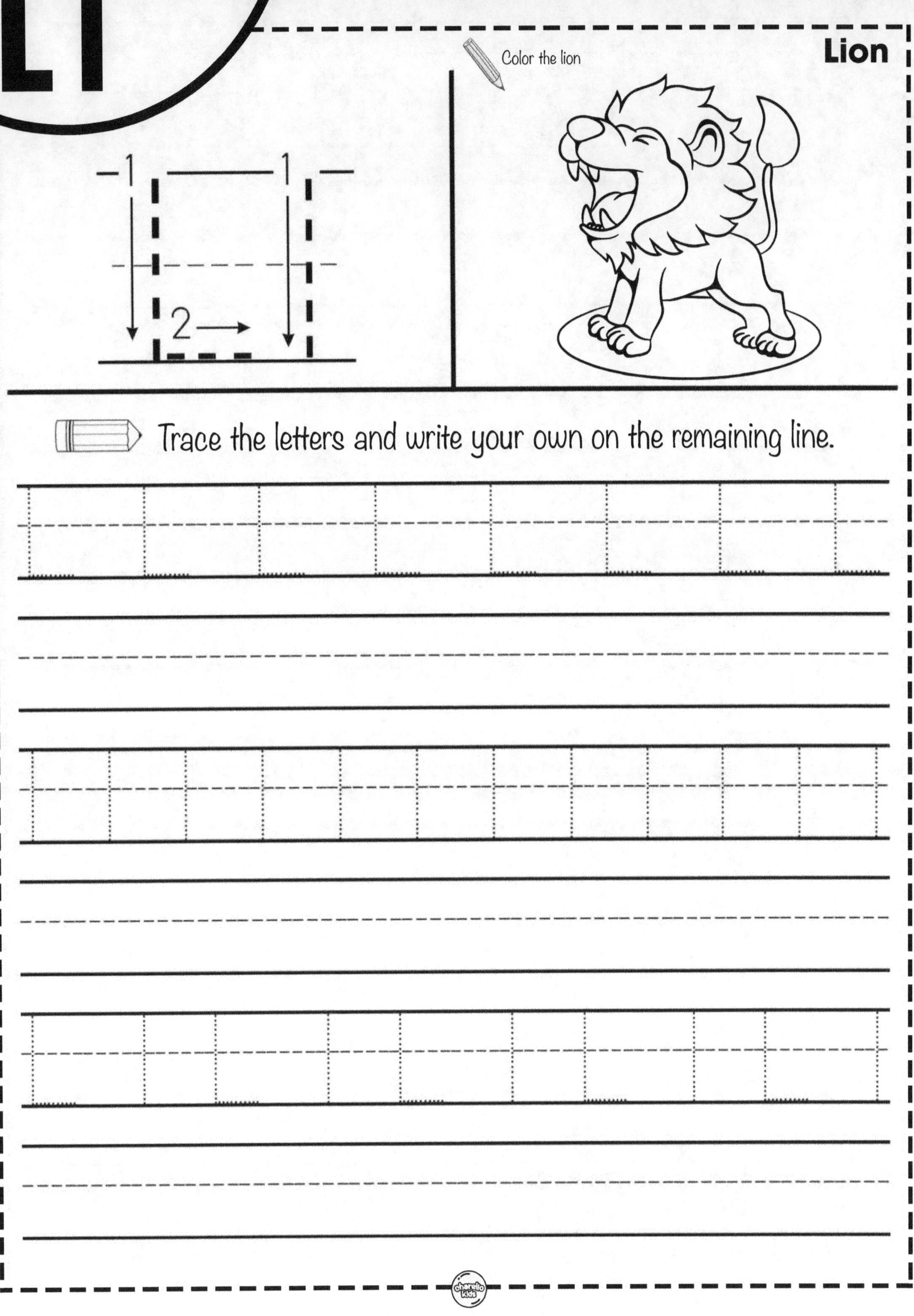

Color the lion
Lion
1
1
2
Trace the letters and write your own on the remaining line.

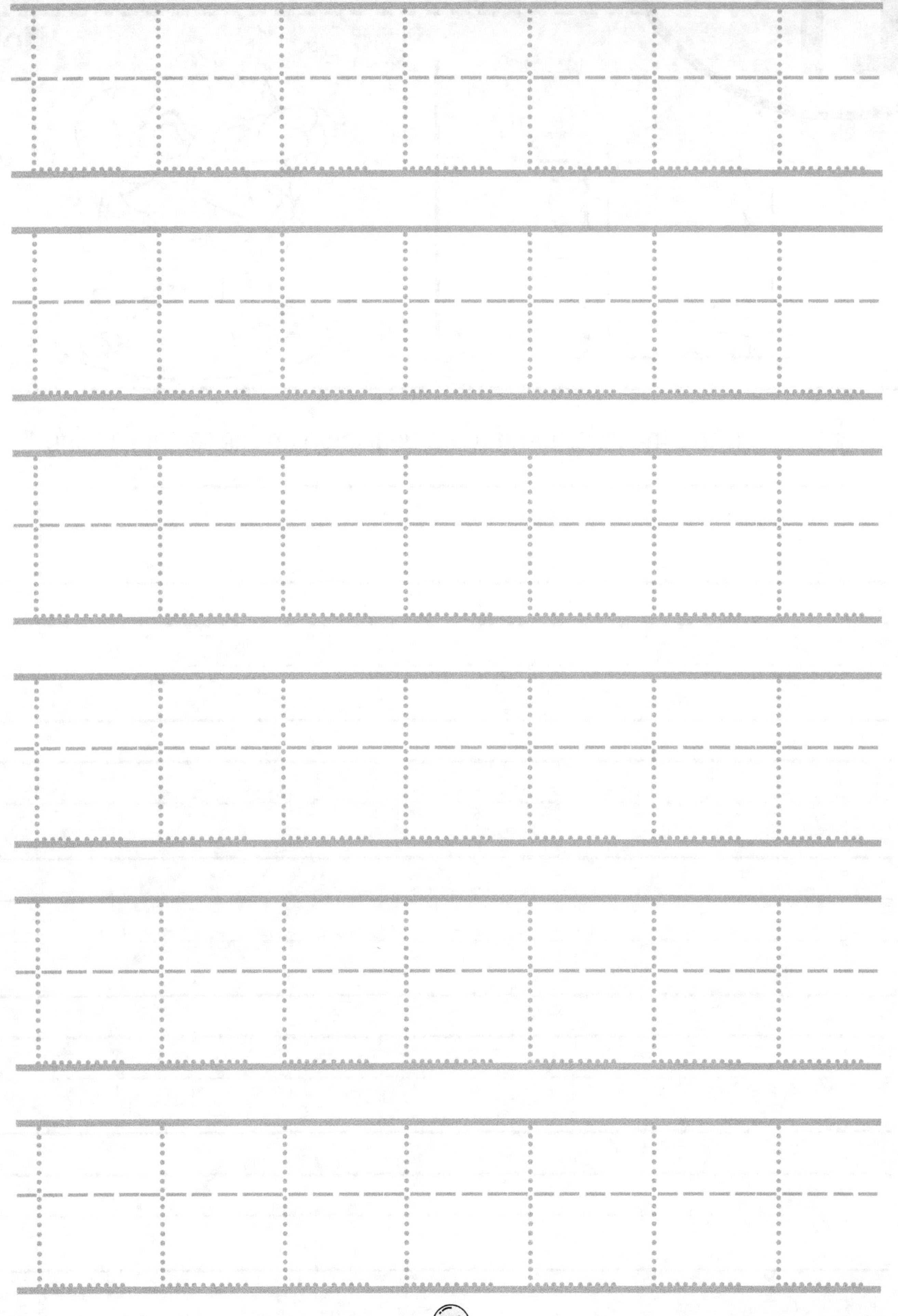

Mm

Color the mailbox

Trace the letters and write your own on the remaining line.

M   M   M   M   M   M   M   M

m   m   m   m   m   m   m

M   m   M   m   m   M   m

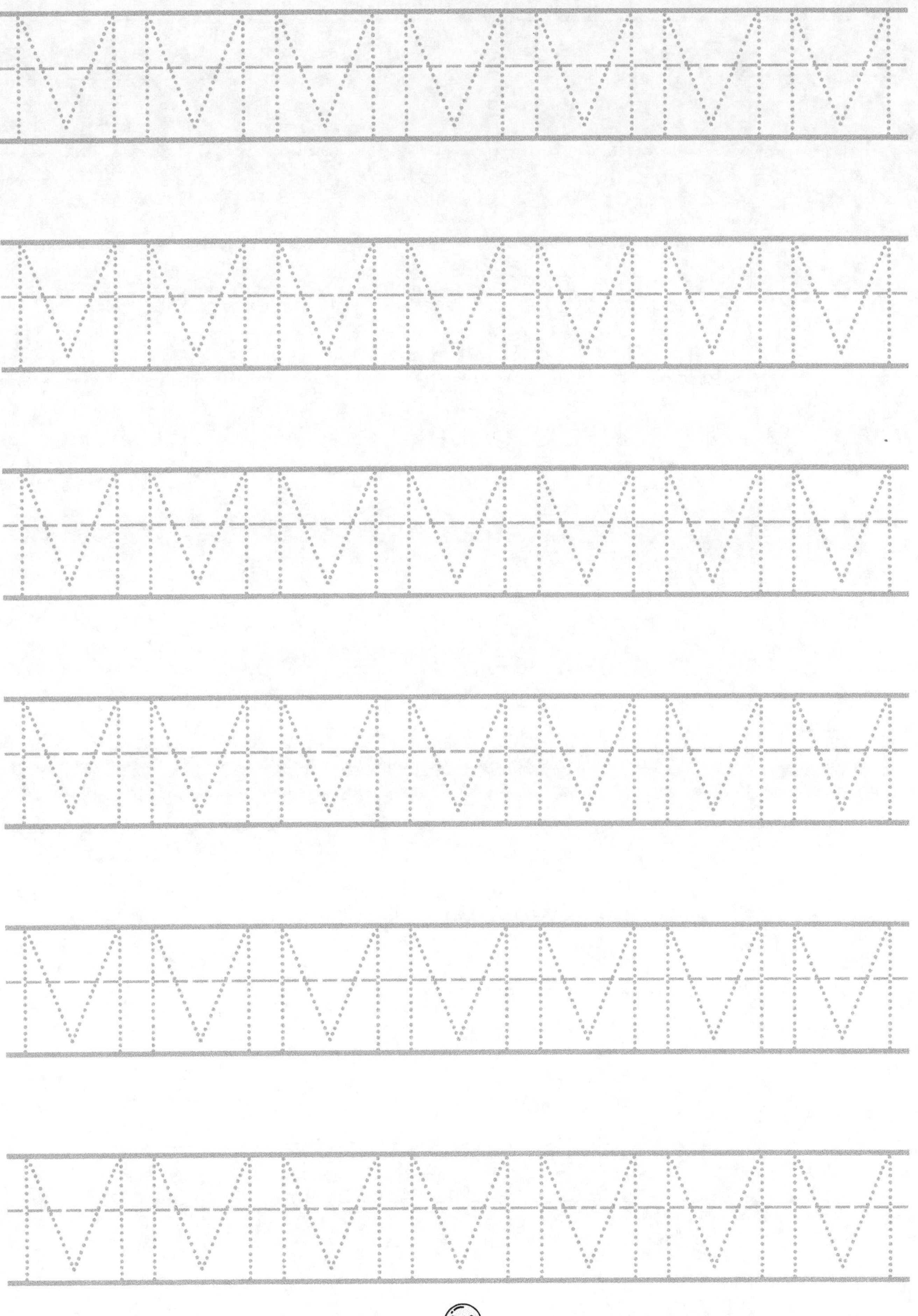

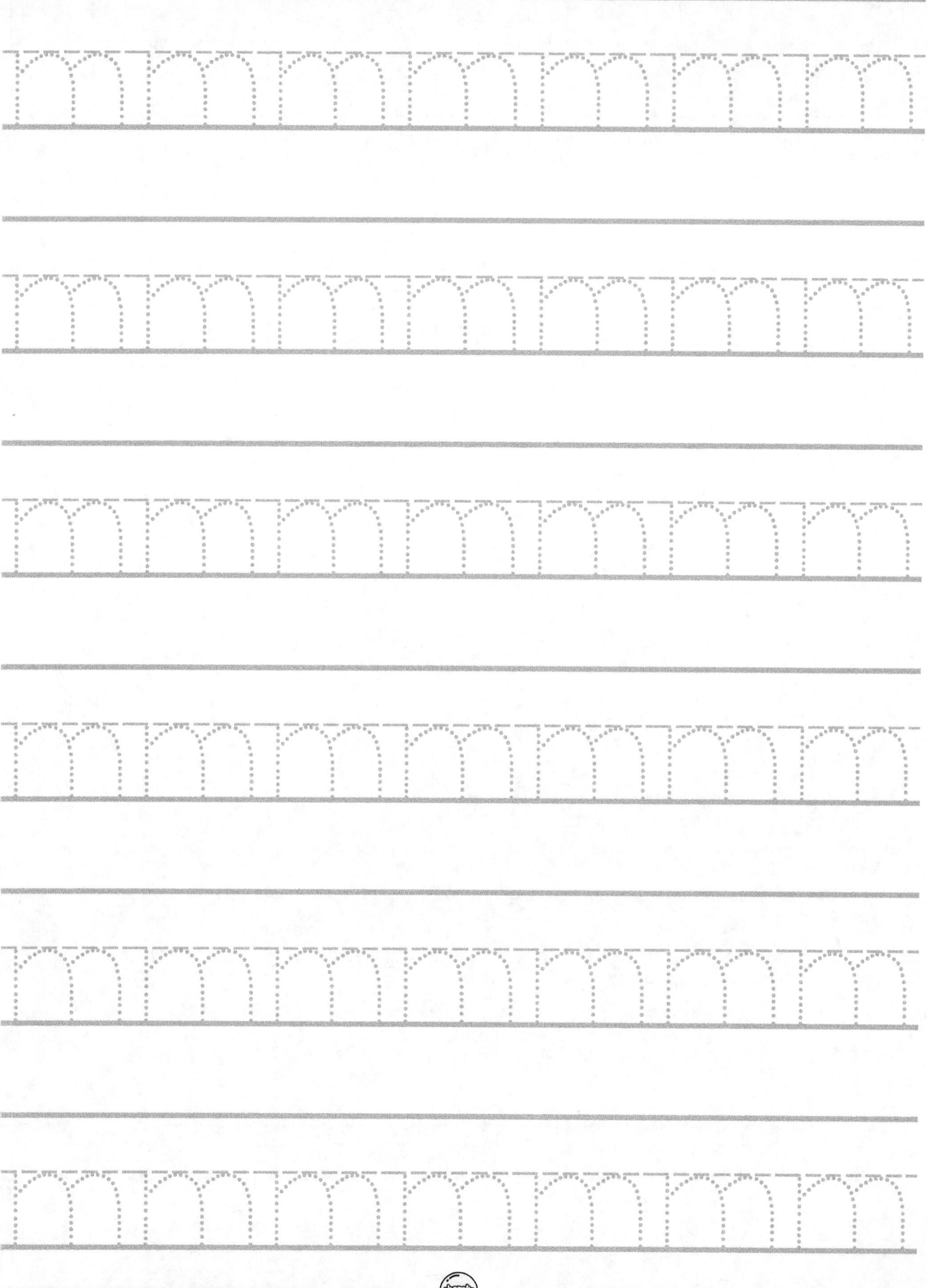

Nn

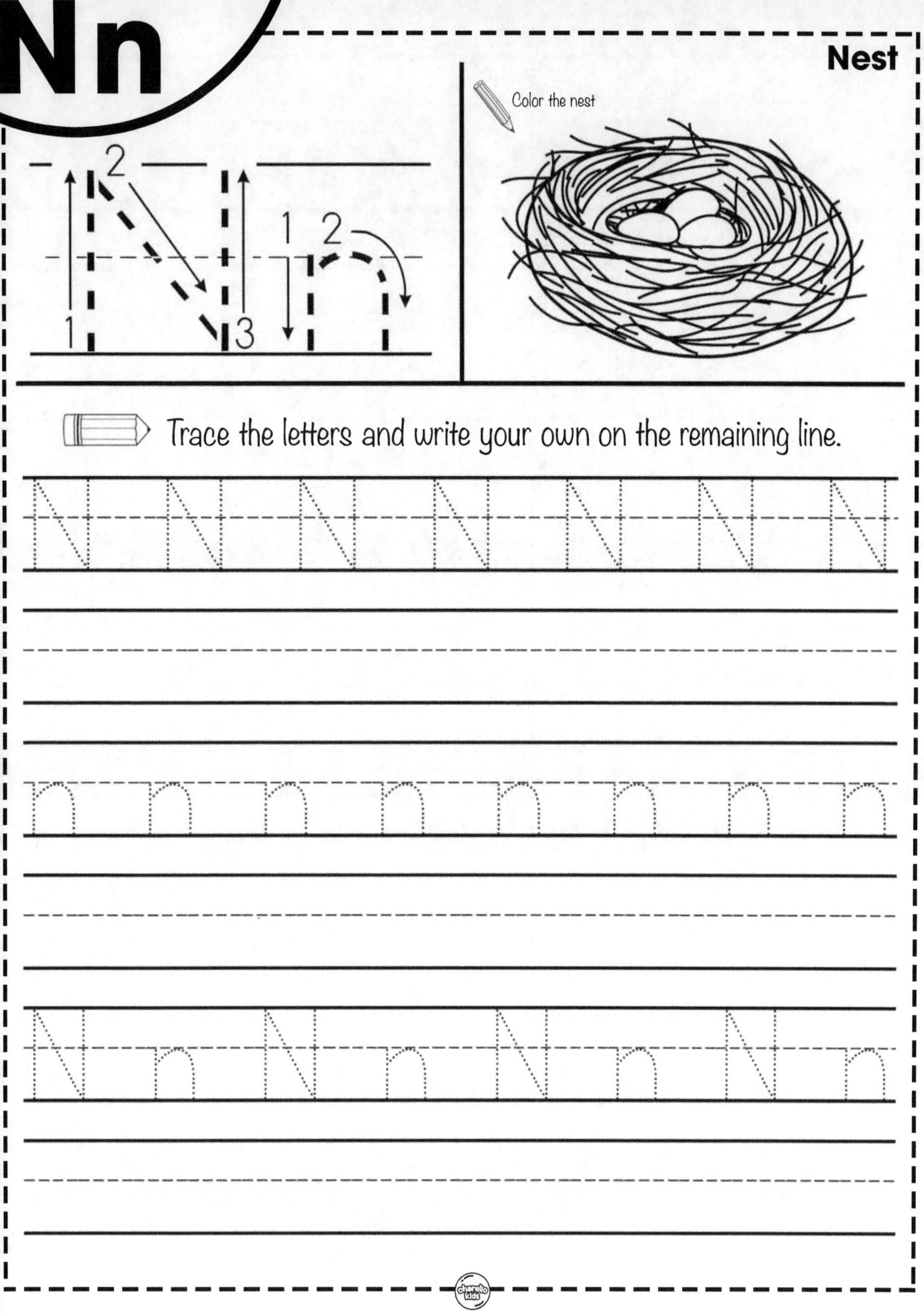

Trace the letters and write your own on the remaining line.

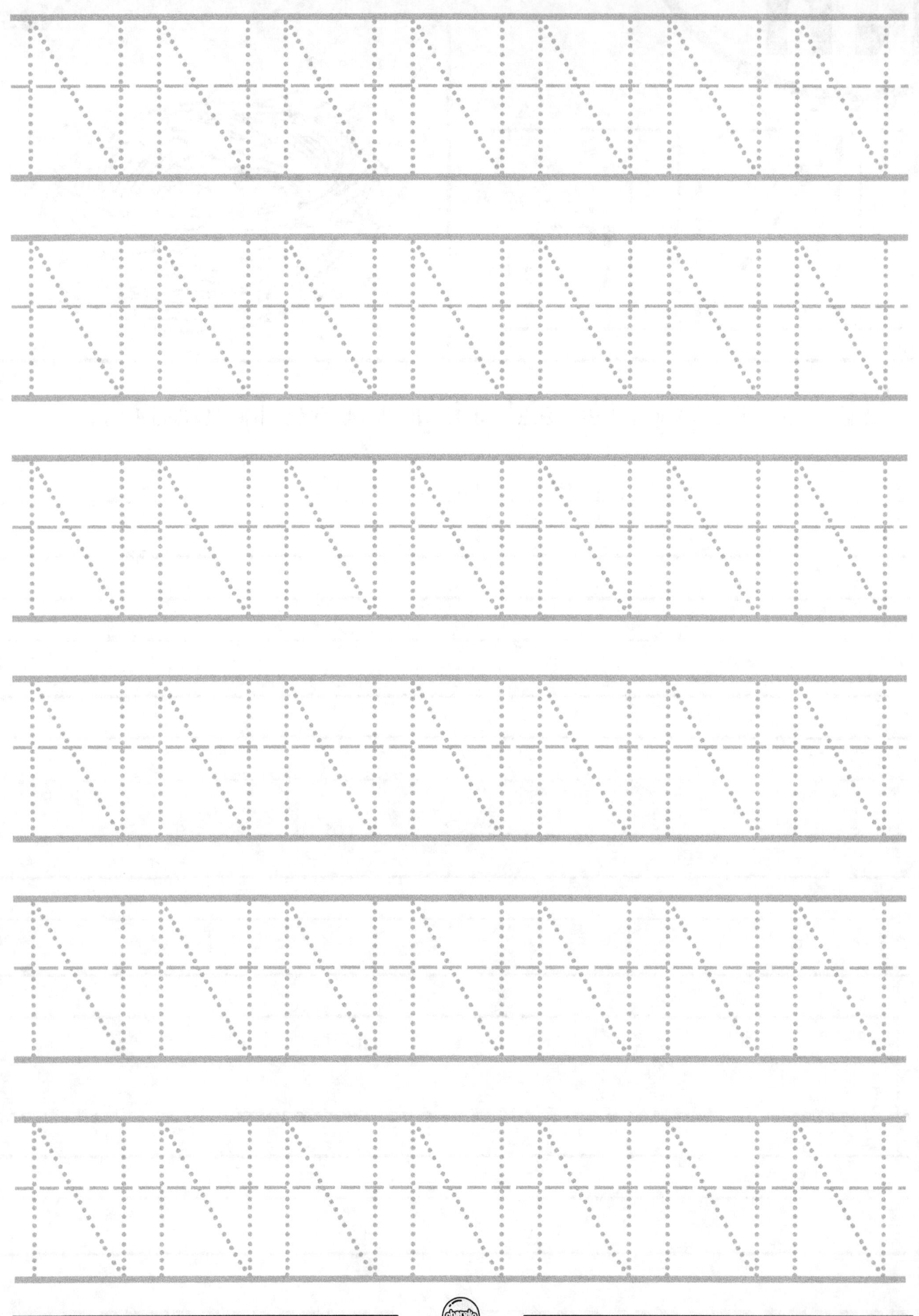

Oo

Color the octopus

1

1

Trace the letters and write your own on the remaining line.

Pp

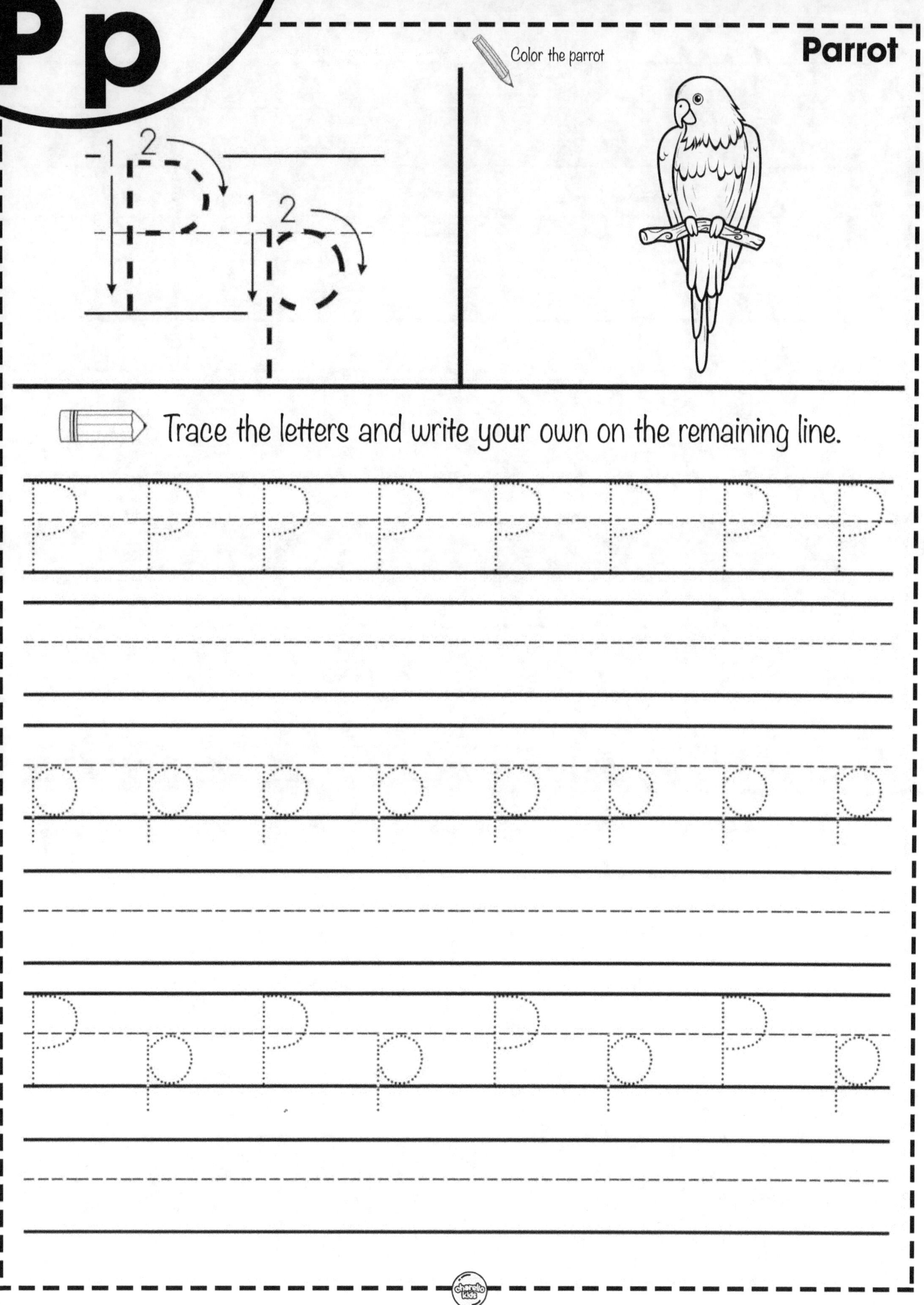

Color the parrot
Parrot
Trace the letters and write your own on the remaining line.

Qq

Trace the letters and write your own on the remaining line.

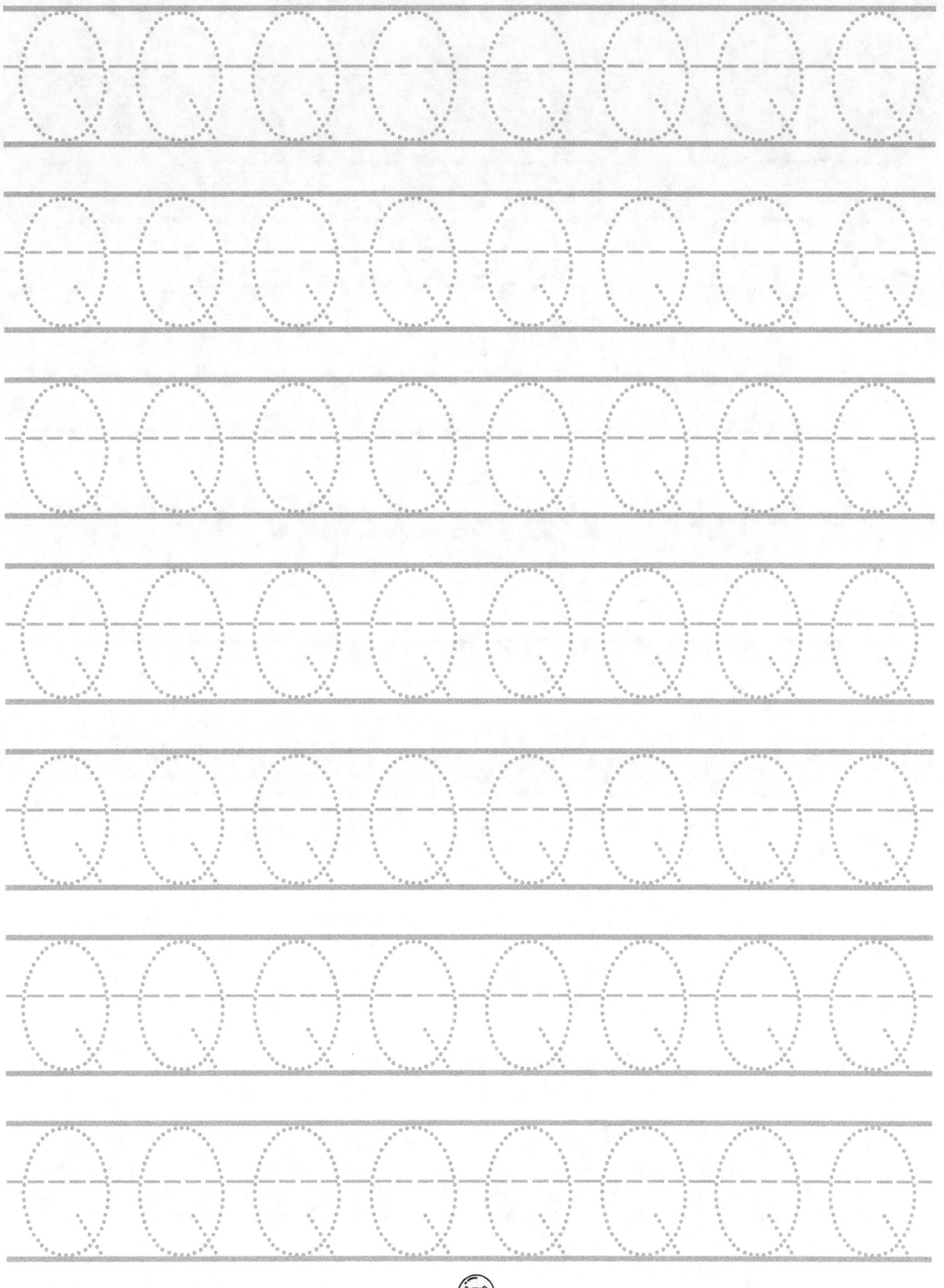

R r

Trace the letters and write your own on the remaining line.

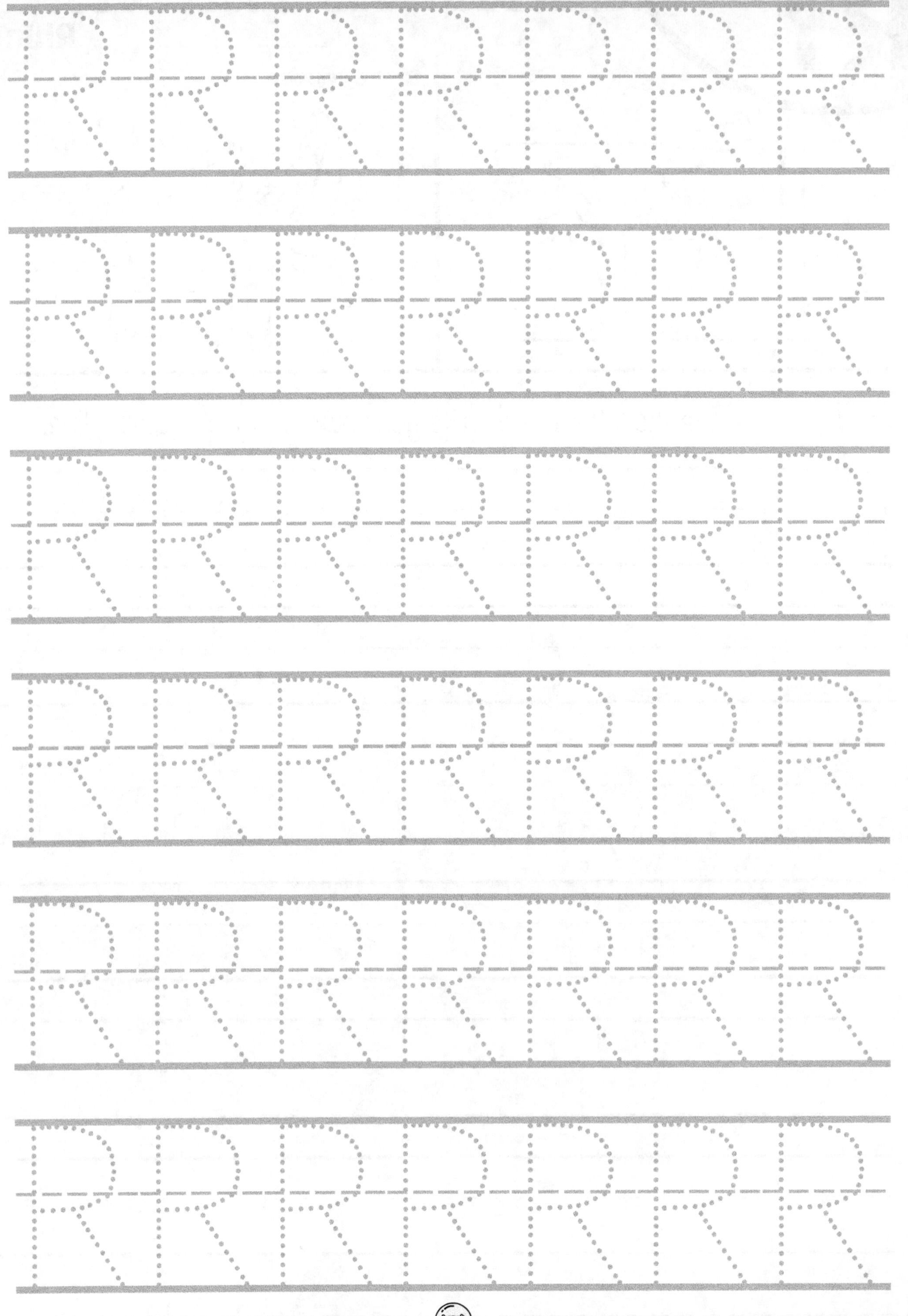

Ss

Sheep
Color the sheep
Trace the letters and write your own on the remaining line.

Cherello
kids

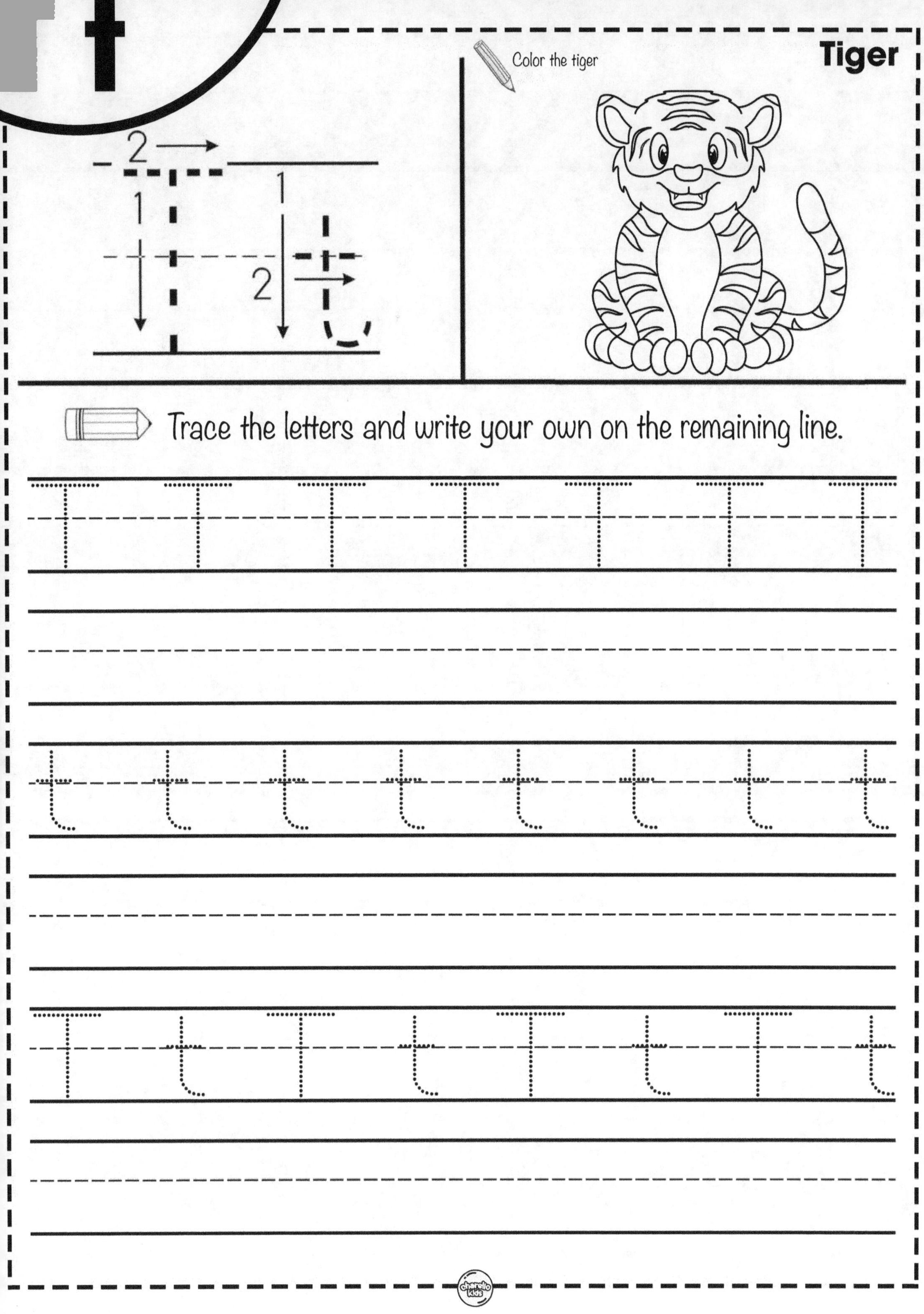

Trace the letters and write your own on the remaining line.

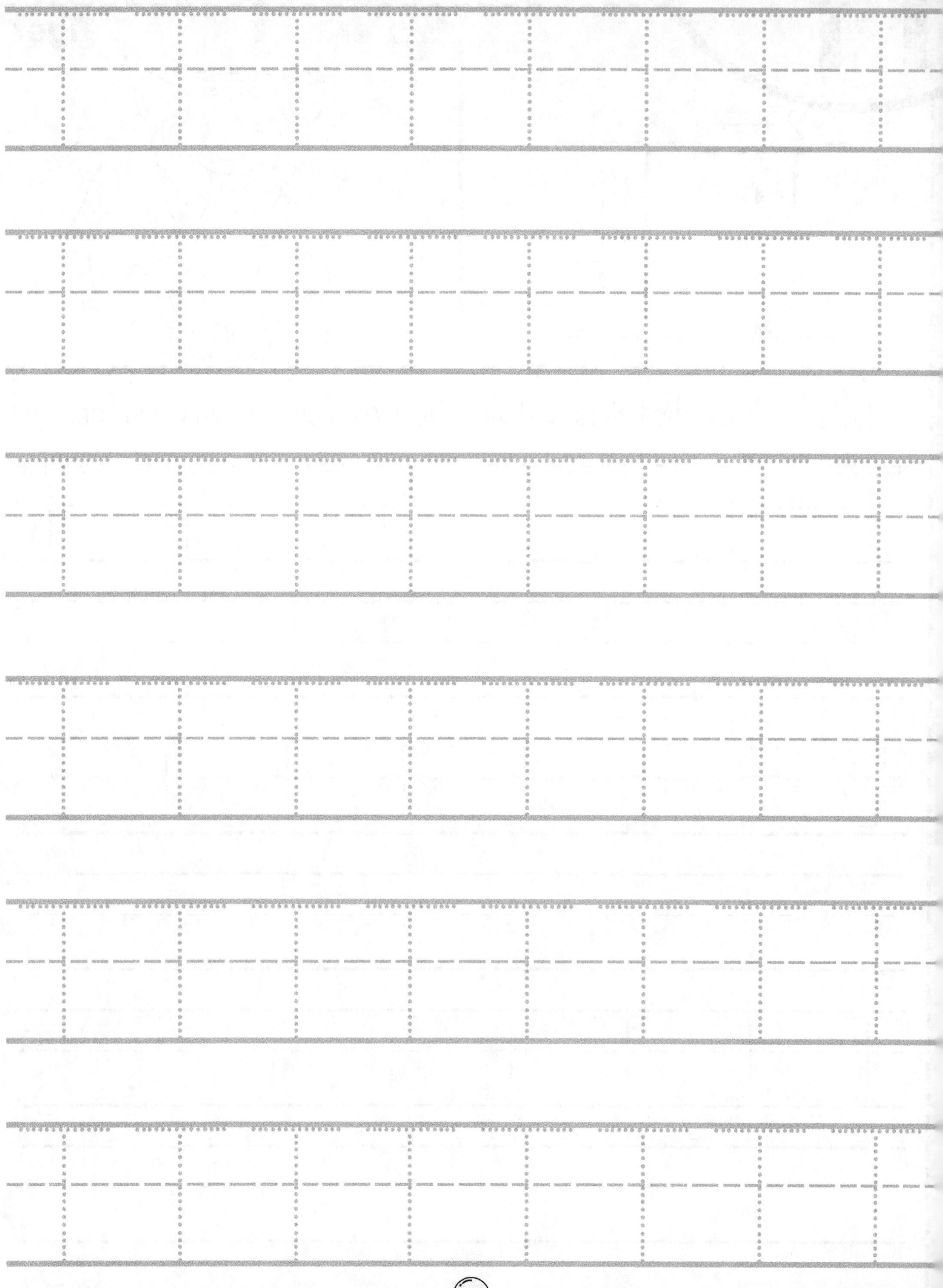

Uu

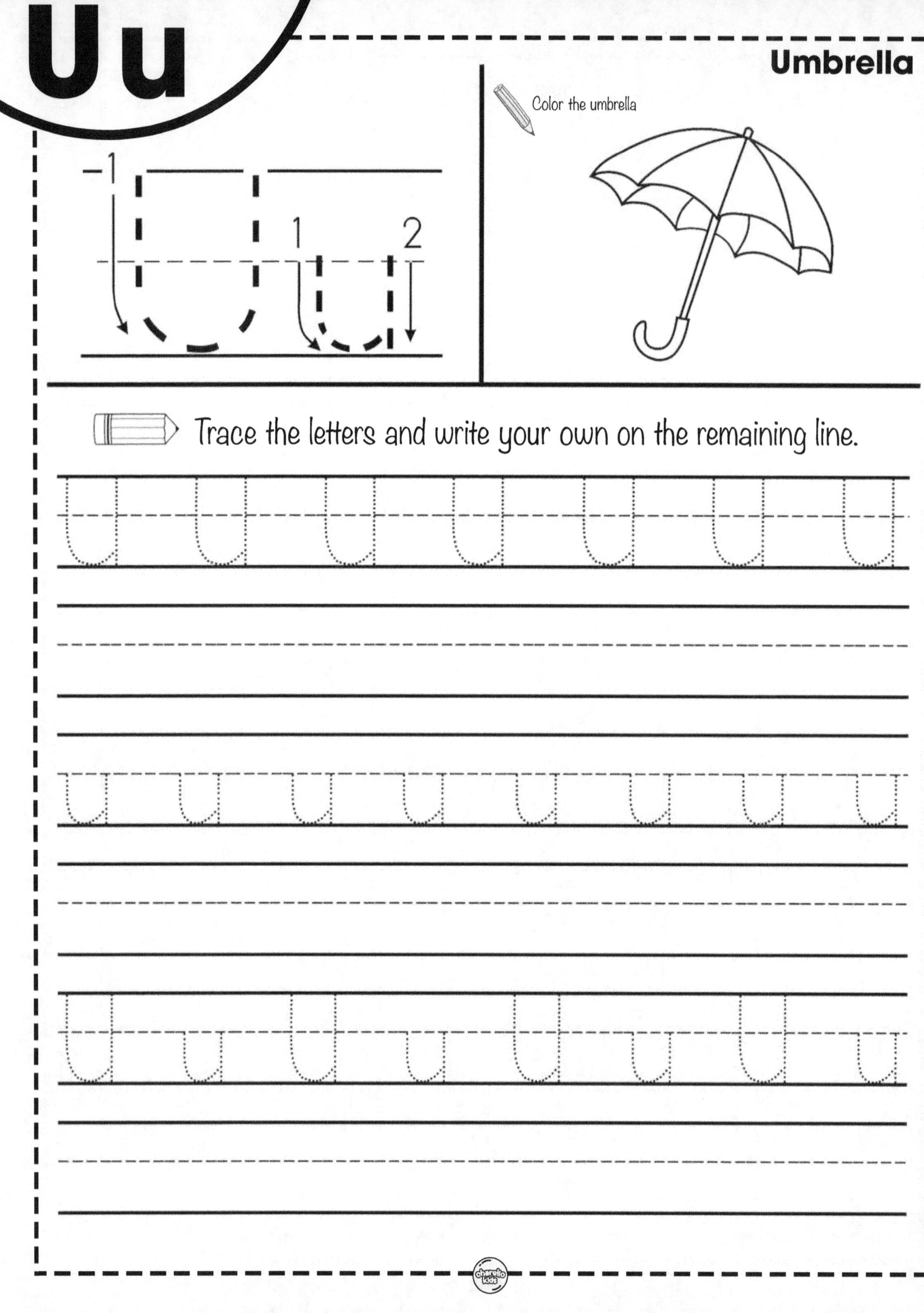

Color the umbrella

Trace the letters and write your own on the remaining line.

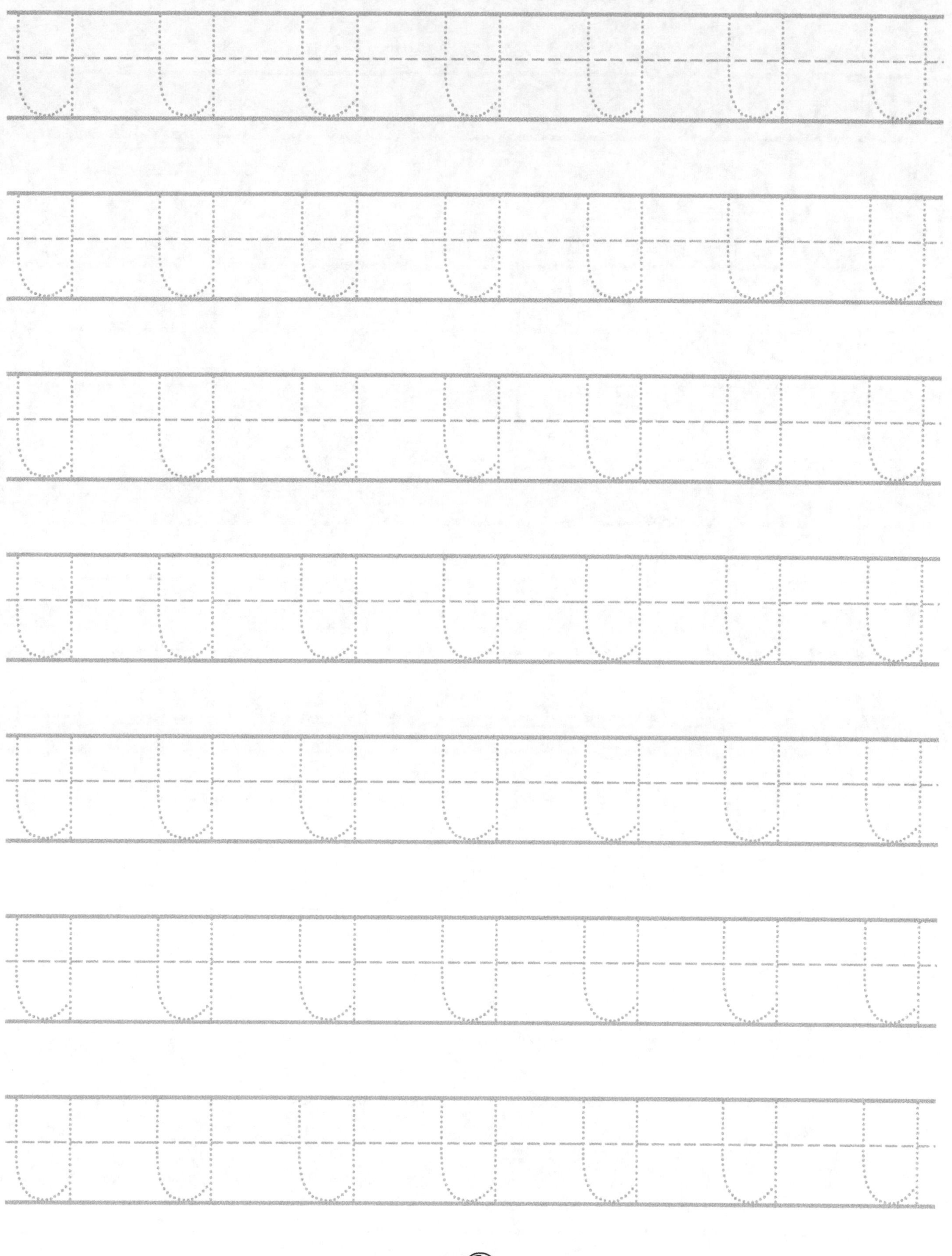

Vv

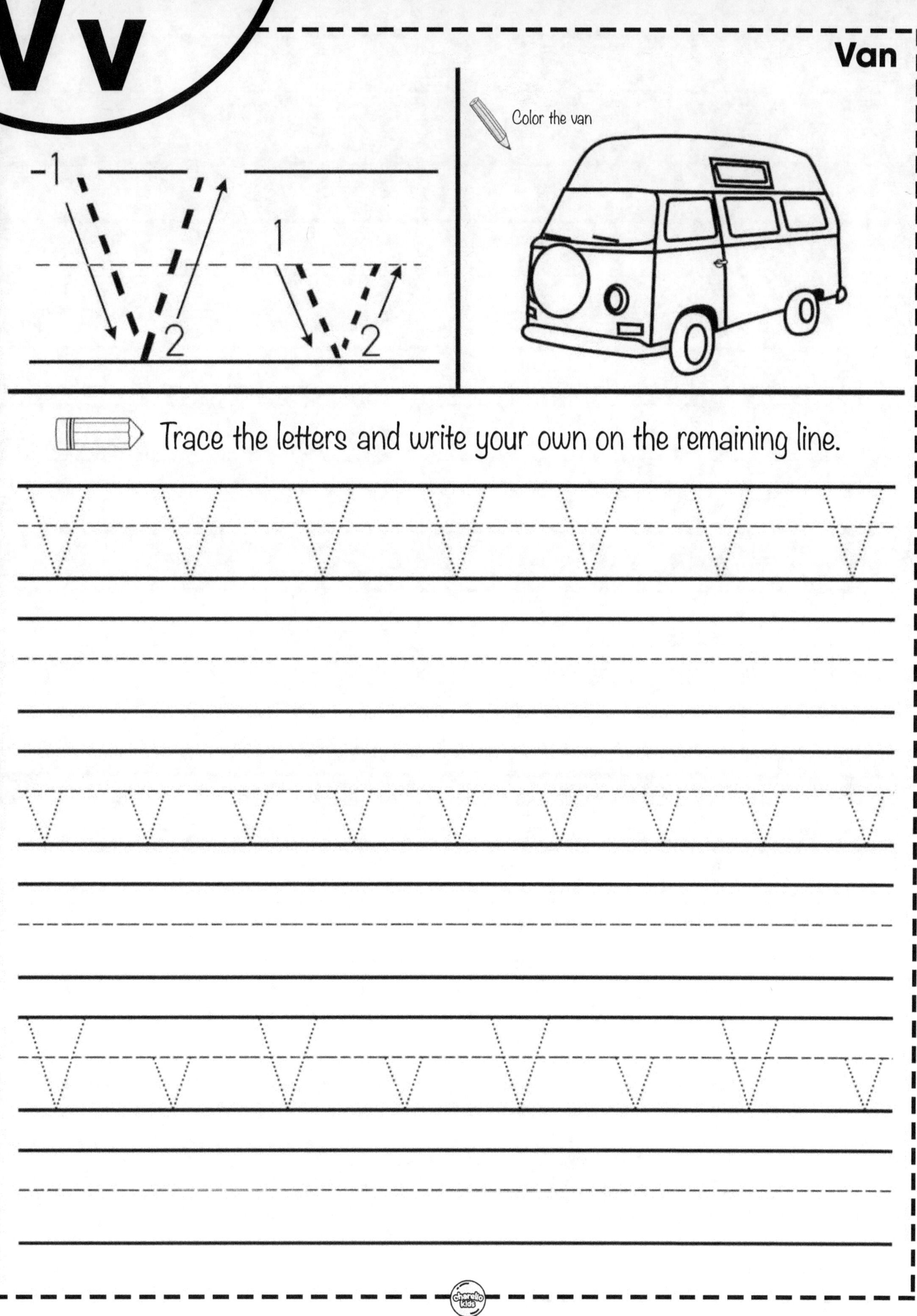

Trace the letters and write your own on the remaining line.

Ww
Whale
Color the whale
Trace the letters and write your own on the remaining line.

Xx

Xylophone
Color the xylophone
Trace the letters and write your own on the remaining line.

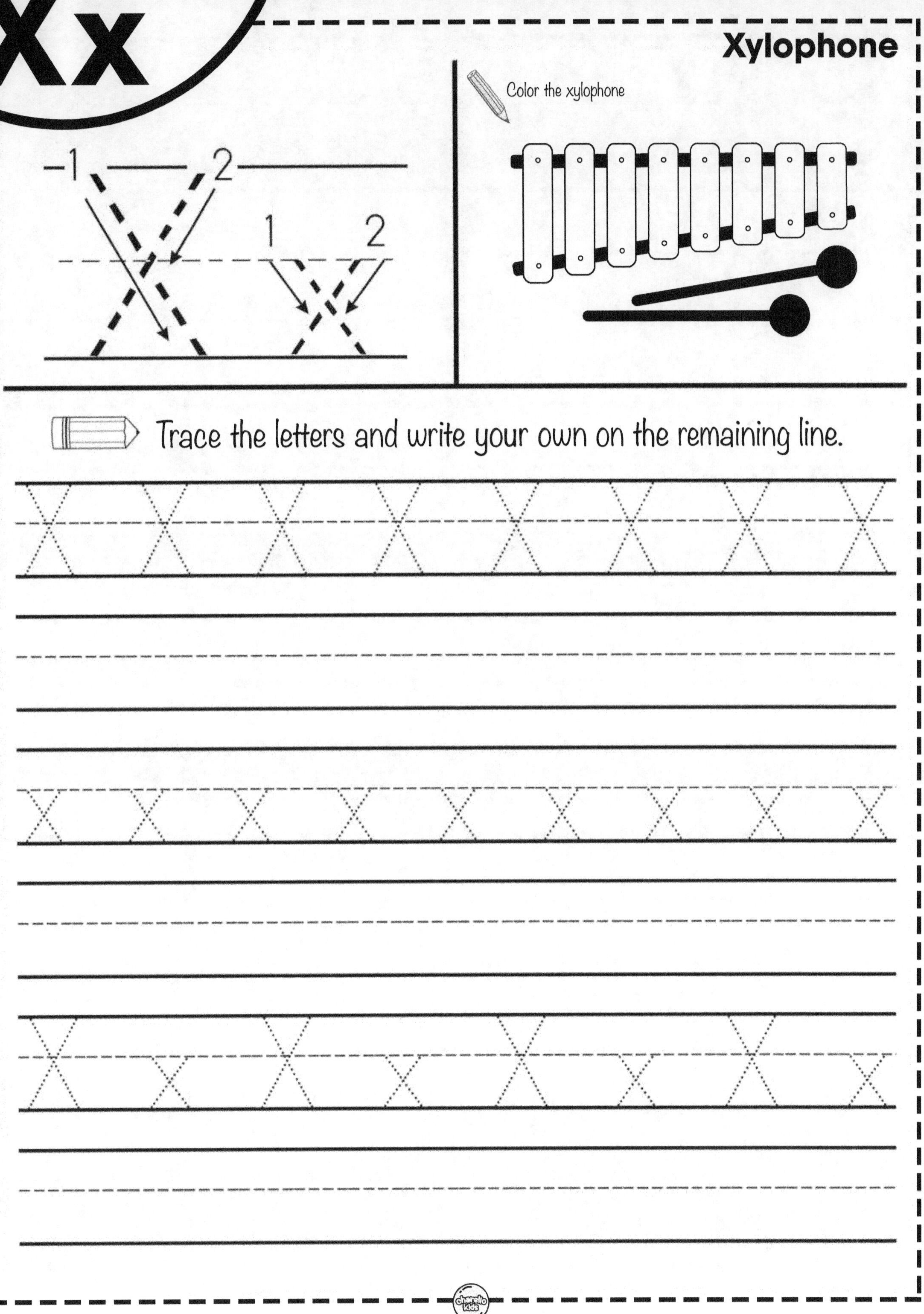

X X X X X X X X X

X X X X X X X X X

X X X X X X X X X

X X X X X X X X X

X X X X X X X X X

X X X X X X X X X

Yy
Yak
Color the yak
Trace the letters and write your own on the remaining line.

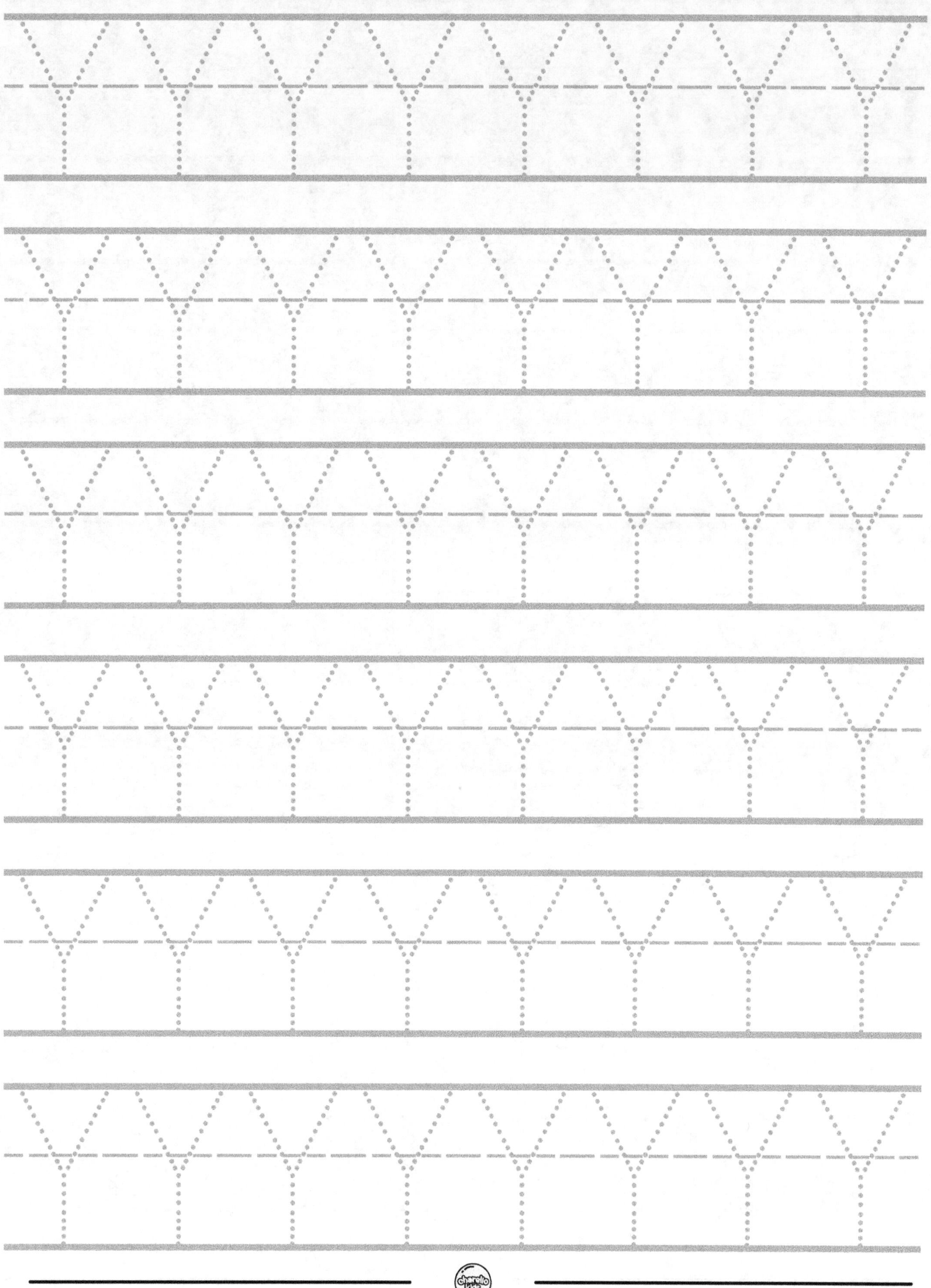

Zz

1

1

Color the zebra

Trace the letters and write your own on the remaining line.

charelio
kids

If you have any questions or suggestions,
we look forward to your message:
feedback@charello-kids.com

Imprint: HEISE Marketing und Werbung · Neddener Dorfstr. 49 · 27308 Kirchlinteln · Germany
E-Mail: publisher@charello-kids.com · www.charello-kids.com